WHEN YOU DON'T KNOW WHAT TO DO

Trusting Christ When Life Gets Confusing

Small Group Leader's Guide

CONTENTS

Introduction	3
The 50-Day Adventure in Small Groups	6
The Role of the Small Group Facilitator	8
Small Group Covenant	10
Getting Started	12
Session 1	14
Session 2	20
Session 3	26
Session 4	32
Session 5	36
Session 6	42
Session 7	50
Session 8	56
Last Words	62
Small Group Resources	63
Order Form	64

Written by Marilyn Moravec
Editor: Brian Hayes
Adventure Series Editor: Marian Oliver
Cover Illustration: Joe VanSeveren
Cover Design: Tony Laidig
Text Design: Blum Graphic Design

Copyright © 1995 *The Chapel Ministries, Inc.*
Published by *The Chapel Ministries*
Dr. David R. Mains, Director

All rights reserved. Sessions 1–8 may be reproduced for use by members of a single small group only. Each small group facilitator should have a complete copy of this book. Permission to reproduce anything other than Sessions 1–8 should be submitted in writing to The Chapel Ministries, Box 30, Wheaton, IL 60189-0030, (708) 668-7292.

All Scripture quotations, unless otherwise indicated, are taken from the HOLY BIBLE, NEW INTERNATIONAL VERSION®. NIV® Copyright ©1973, 1978, 1984 by International Bible Society. Used by permission of Zondervan Publishing House. All rights reserved.

Scripture quotations marked NASB are from the New American Standard Bible. Copyright ©1960, 1962, 1963, 1968, 1971, 1972, 1973, 1975, and 1977 by The Lockman Foundation. Used by permission.

Scripture quotations from THE MESSAGE are used by permission of NavPress Publishing Group. Copyright ©1993

Scripture quotations marked "The Amplified Bible" are from The Amplified New Testament, copyright © 1954, 1958, 1987 by The Lockman Foundation. Used by permission.

Material in "The Role of the Small Group Facilitator" is adapted from *Getting along with People You Love* by Marilyn Moravec. Copyright © 1989 by David C. Cook Publishing Co. Used by permission.

The Chapel Ministries is a nonprofit, nondenominational, international Christian outreach dedicated to helping God's church grow spiritually and numerically by revitalizing its members, whether they be gathered or scattered, to be a force for kingdom purposes worldwide. To support this goal, The Chapel Ministries provides print and media resources including the annual 50-Day Spiritual Adventure and 4-Week Worship Celebration, the daily half-hour television program "You Need to Know," and seasonal radio programming. Year-round Bible study guides are offered through a Joint Ministry Venture with Scripture Union U.S.A., to encourage the healthy spiritual habits of daily Scripture reading and prayer.

Printed in the United States of America

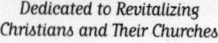

ISBN 1-879050-75-7

INTRODUCTION

Welcome to the 50-Day Spiritual Adventure team! Whether you're an experienced small group leader or a novice, you'll find the Adventure to be a wonderful vehicle for spiritual growth and group interaction.

This Small Group Leader's Guide contains the essential helps you'll need to successfully lead a group of adventurers in your church, neighborhood, workplace, or school on a time of discovery and growth.

The 50-Day Adventure is an annual event—a time when hundreds of thousands of believers across North America work together on basic disciplines of the Christian faith, including Bible study, prayer, and service. In fact, we're hoping that close to one million people will participate in 1996.

Each of the Adventure studies is developed around a central topic, and this year's study will have a powerful impact on its participants. Titled "What to Do When You Don't Know What to Do: Trusting Christ When Life Gets Confusing," the Adventure includes eight themes and five action steps (spiritual disciplines).

How can we make it through the confusing situations in our lives? The eight themes prepare us to face our times of doubt and disorientation with the promises, joys, and guidance of Jesus Christ.

Before You Begin

The Adventure is unique in that it can be used by individuals and small groups as well as by entire church congregations.

The Adventure is seven weeks (eight Sundays) in length. In settings where an entire congregation participates, the eight Adventure themes become the pastor's preaching themes for the eight Sundays of the series. In this Small Group Leader's Guide there are eight sessions, one for each theme of the Adventure.

Most people will be using the Adventure material from Sunday, February 18, through Easter Sunday, April 7, 1996. However, the material is completely undated, so it can be used during any eight-Sunday period you choose.

Individual Adventure participants will receive a complete introduction to the eight topics and five Adventure action steps on pages 3–12 in the Adult Journal. As a small group leader, you will want to familiarize yourself with the journal to gain an overall understanding of the Adventure. You will also want to read *When Life Becomes a Maze: Discovering Christ's Resources for Times of Confusion* by David Mains for further insight into the eight Adventure topics. (See below for more information.)

Keep in mind that what we're presenting here is only a springboard for you. Yes, the model for the weekly meeting plans has been tested in small groups for a number of years. But don't be afraid to be creative! Trust your instincts and your own knowledge of your group members. If something works well, keep with it. If not, adjust and adapt the materials until you feel comfortable.

If the first thing you're confused about is leading a small group study, you'll be pleased to find that this guide contains introductory information on small groups as well as specific helps for facilitators.

So, are you ready to get underway? In addition to your Bible and a solid undergirding of prayer, the following is an outline of the basic Adventure materials you and your group members will find helpful.

Key Resources

Adult Journal. This is an absolutely essential resource for individuals following the Adventure on a daily basis. Each journal contains a biblical examination of the Adventure topics, information on the five Adventure action steps, and a place to complete all the daily assignments. Having a journal is not a requirement for small group participation, but group members will get much more out of the Adventure if they use the daily journal.

When Life Becomes a Maze: Discovering Christ's Resources for Times of Confusion by David Mains is also a necessary item, especially for small group leaders. This 190-page Adventure guidebook devotes one chapter to each topic of the Adventure. Designed to provide motivation and added insights for the Adventure experience, this book is full of illustrations and practical suggestions. (Available as an audiobook also.)

***Believe It Or Not* Scripture Promise Pack.** This handy mini-pack provides Scripture verses to help your group members embrace God's promises. The 16 selections are all related to the Adventure and will give people ready access to God's comforting words in confusing times.

The Adventure Orientation Video. This 85-minute video is an excellent tool for explaining the Adventure concept and action steps to your small group. It may be viewed in segments or all together. Including a brief overview of the 50-Day Spiritual Adventure, Chapel Ministries staff and guests discuss Adventure topics and action steps, and Chapel Director David Mains shares his passion to see God work through the local church.

Part 2 of the video is dedicated to explaining the enhanced aspects of the Adventure. These sections will show you specific ways to best implement the Adventure in your small group.

The Adventure Resource Video contains eight short dramas plus selected clips from the "You Need to Know" television program. Use these segments as ice-breakers, to stimulate discussion, or to introduce Adventure topics.

"You Need to Know" is another resource that may be of interest to your group. This half-hour weekday television program addresses the Adventure topics with interesting guests and round-table discussions. For a broadcast schedule, contact The Chapel Ministries.

These resources and other Adventure materials may be ordered from The Chapel Ministries, Box 30, Wheaton, Illinois 60189. Use the order form on page 64. Or simply call our office weekdays toll-free at:
1-800-224-2735 (U.S.)   1-800-461-4114 (Canada)

IMPORTANT: To ensure that you receive materials in time to begin the Adventure with your group, we suggest you place your order at least one month in advance—earlier, if at all possible. For fastest delivery, use our toll-free order line and your Discover, VISA, or MasterCard.

THE 50-DAY ADVENTURE IN SMALL GROUPS

Why Small Groups?

Think about the early church. New Testament believers met in house churches for the breaking of bread, fellowship, and worship. Many churches today also had humble beginnings. And many of the growing churches attribute their success, at least in part, to the ministry of small groups.

A Gallup poll taken in a large Protestant denomination revealed that for 52 percent of the people the small group was the support system for their faith. Another survey indicated that 40 to 70 percent of new people were assimilated into the church through small groups, often at a time when they needed support to deal with a challenging life situation.

Small groups are the logical setting for building community. Individuals can get lost in larger churches. They may feel intimidated by those who are public speakers. Deeper levels of sharing and open lines of communication occur best in small groups. This is where individual needs can be mentioned and strangers can become friends.

By definition, small groups are an excellent medium for teaching and discipling. Because of their caring and people-centered nature, they are also fertile soil for evangelism. Those grappling with the message of salvation can be encouraged. Mature believers find support and encouragement and challenge.

What are some other advantages? Small groups are flexible enough to adjust if necessary; they occur in a natural and personal environment; and they are layperson-led in a nonthreatening atmosphere.

What Is a Small Group?

A small group is a gathering of four to twelve (eight being optimum) who come together on a regular—usually weekly—basis to support one another and to grow spiritually.

Many formats can be used—Bible study groups, prayer circles, accountability groups, or support groups. Other names may be used (such as cell groups), but the primary purpose is to help Christians mature spiritually.

The shared intimacy of a small group Christian fellowship can be the ideal place to learn and to sense the will of God. It is a place for loving and learning, teaching and training, and prayer and praise. Further, with a format of Bible study, fellowship, worship, and mission, the small group can be the greatest setting for developing one's spiritual gifts.

Can the 50-Day Spiritual Adventure be effectively used with small groups? Can the materials be adapted for use in home Bible studies, Sunday school classes, or a gathering of friends?

Absolutely! What better place is there to develop a sense of trust than in a small, caring, loving fellowship of believers? What better avenue is there to find direction in the midst of our own anxieties in a world that appears to be spinning madly out of control?

With the Adult Journal as the primary resource, the Adventure is designed to be used by individuals and small groups as well as entire church congregations.

Objectives of a Small Group

The objectives of small groups and what we want to accomplish through the Adventure are virtually identical:
1. To relate ourselves to Christ and his plan for our lives
2. To promote the disciplines of personal prayer and Bible study
3. To provide a format for developing our spiritual gifts
4. To promote a spiritual climate in the areas where we live (local church, home, community)
5. To develop a close, honest, sharing fellowship with others
6. To create an impact in the world through specific service to others

Elements of an Effective Small Group

Russell Robinson, in *Dynamics of Group Leadership*, lists the four essential elements which are the minimum requirements for the formation of any stable group: acceptance, communication, structure, and purpose.

Acceptance provides a sense of security and trust for the participants. It's important for them to feel respect, recognition, and value.

Where **communication** lines are open, individuals can more freely share their values, beliefs, opinions, joys, and frustrations.

Some sort of **structure** is necessary to keep the small group focused. There must be flexibility and freedom on the one hand, but also some control.

Finally, for a small group to be effective, the group must have a **purpose**, and the individual members must understand that goal.

A healthy group exudes acceptance, warmth, joy, nurture, and community. (Milwaukee: Omni Book Co., 1979)

THE ROLE OF THE SMALL GROUP FACILITATOR

What Is a Facilitator?

This material is designed to be led by a facilitator, not a teacher. The material itself will guide you through each session. The word *facilitate* means "to make easier." The most important function of a facilitator is to help create an atmosphere of openness, warmth, and acceptance of one another. This will assist the process of personal growth for each group member, as well as deepen your fellowship. The main asset of the facilitator is his or her own life and desire to change and grow. The facilitator is a fellow member of the group with his or her own needs, who has the additional responsibility of keeping the group on target and watching the time.

One of the main challenges for the facilitator will be to help both the "overtalkers" and "undertalkers" move toward healthy participation in the group discussions. Periodically challenge the group as a whole to move toward change by telling them: "Quiet people push yourself to share; those who share easily, discipline yourself to spend more time listening."

Occasionally you will have someone in the group with great needs. It's best that these be met outside the group time. Make arrangements to meet that person for coffee later so you can hear and respond to those needs. The responsibility of the facilitator is to keep a balance between meeting individual needs and making sure each lesson is covered. Pray for wisdom! When the discussion has slid into a tangent, it's best to take charge and tell the group, "We need to get back to the questions." Also, remember to contact absentees with a note or phone call before the next meeting.

These lessons can be done without preparation by group members. Adventurers will be concentrating on completing their daily journals during the week, so it may be best not to hand out group sessions prior to your meetings. The sessions in this guide may be reproduced for your group members. We encourage you to do that each week.

If you have people in your group who are not familiar with the Scriptures, provide Bibles and use page numbers to make it easier for them to find the passages. You should be able to obtain inexpensive Bibles through your local Christian bookstore. Or, contact the International Bible Society at 1-800-524-1588.

How to Facilitate the Group

The most important thing to know about facilitating this Adventure series is that the material in this guide will lead you through the group time. Instructions to the group and/or facilitator are placed within the material itself—in *italic* type. You can read through the session aloud and answer the questions as you come to them. The study questions are designed in such a way that they can be answered as you move through the material together.

Begin the group by reading the material aloud, or by asking a volunteer to do so. As you work through each session, have every section and all Scripture passages read aloud by volunteers.

Notice that the question numbers function primarily as thematic section markers. Thus, not all questions are numbered. For instance, number one may give a paragraph or two of informational material before actually raising a question to be answered in the blank space. Then there may be two or three more follow-up questions without numbers—since those questions still relate to the theme or idea in number one.

Do not call on anyone to read or share. All sharing should be voluntary. You'll discover that quiet people can be great growers. Verbal ability is not necessarily a sign of life change. Do not try to force openness. Instead, model it. On the questions where the instruction is given to go around the group, begin yourself and share in a way that will encourage others to follow your lead. This means you must be willing to be candid, open, and vulnerable. This is scary, but worth it in terms of helping the group move toward deeper levels of relating.

Most sessions end in group prayer. Do not go around the group for this, unless specifically directed otherwise. Allow those who wish to just listen to be comfortable, and those who wish to pray aloud to do so. Explain that sentence prayer is best in small groups, especially new or young groups; encourage members to simply talk to the Lord. Close the prayer time yourself or ask for a volunteer to close.

Prepare to facilitate the group by completing each session ahead of time. The other most important preparation is prayer. Pray specifically for each person in your group as well as for yourself, that God will be free to accomplish his goals in each of your lives.

SMALL GROUP COVENANT

Many groups begin with a covenant or contract. This is simply a statement of the group's purpose and the general means by which it intends to achieve that purpose. The covenant establishes intention, defines expectations, provides accountability, enhances commitment, puts love into action, and establishes ground rules. The group rules anticipate questions regarding refreshments, baby-sitting, newcomers, and absences.

A sample small group covenant follows. You may use it as a model for a covenant of your own, allowing those in your group to tailor the document to your specific needs.

Small Group Covenant

The purpose of our group is to provide a warm and accepting fellowship where all members of the group may share and feel cared for. Further, we hope to grow in godly wisdom through worship, study, and service. Specifically, we purpose together to complete the group agenda set forth in our group goals.

Our goals are:
1. To walk through the 50-Day Adventure as a group.
2. To apply the Adventure action steps to our everyday lives as guided by the study.
3. To pray regularly for the Adventure and for our pastor(s) and leaders.
4. To be openly supportive of those within the group, being good listeners, not judging or criticizing, and keeping all that is said in confidence.
5. To regularly attend all designated meetings and to be accountable to the group.

We will meet for eight weeks and decide, toward the end of our study, whether to continue the group.
We will meet on _____ from _____ to _____ P.M./A.M.
We will gather weekly at _____.
We will give group meetings priority in our weekly schedules.
We will practice punctuality, confidentiality, and prayerful support. To these principles we all agree.

Signed:

GETTING STARTED

If your entire congregation is going to be involved in the 50-Day Spiritual Adventure, those in your small group will complete the individual assignments in the Adventure journal, listen to the pastor's message in the context of a weekly worship service, and participate in a weekly small group.

Specifically, each adult will be encouraged to sign up for the Adventure, get a journal, and begin the daily assignments. The pastor will give an orientation to the action steps, explain how to use the journal, and introduce the supplementary books related to the Adventure themes.

Even if your church is not participating in the 50-Day Spiritual Adventure, the materials are well suited for a small group setting. In fact, many Adventure churches are first introduced to the series through the involvement of a Sunday school class or other small group. For groups doing the Adventure "solo," without the benefit of weekly sermons on Adventure topics, it will be doubly important for individuals to go through the companion book *When Life Becomes a Maze* by David Mains. (See the order form on p. 64.) In "solo" groups it is the facilitator's job to orient participants to the journal and action steps.

Choosing the Best Setting

You may use the 50-Day Spiritual Adventure as a series in an existing Bible study. Or you may choose to form a new small group exclusively for the Adventure. The materials have been successfully used by hundreds of small groups in a variety of settings—including neighborhood coffees, Bible studies, adult Sunday school electives, and office Bible studies.

Your small group's agenda will be based on the weekly Adventure themes. Each session is designed to run for 90 minutes. If you don't have that much time available for your small group meetings, the facilitator will need to decide ahead of time which questions to eliminate. Even if you only use some of the questions, we still recommend that you reproduce the sessions in this guide for your group.

If your group grows to more than 12 members, here are two options we suggest. You might birth another group to meet with another facilitator at another location. Or, you could remain in a larger group for part of the meeting. Then when discussion begins, multiply into two groups meeting in separate rooms at the same location. Smaller groups make it easier for quiet members to share.

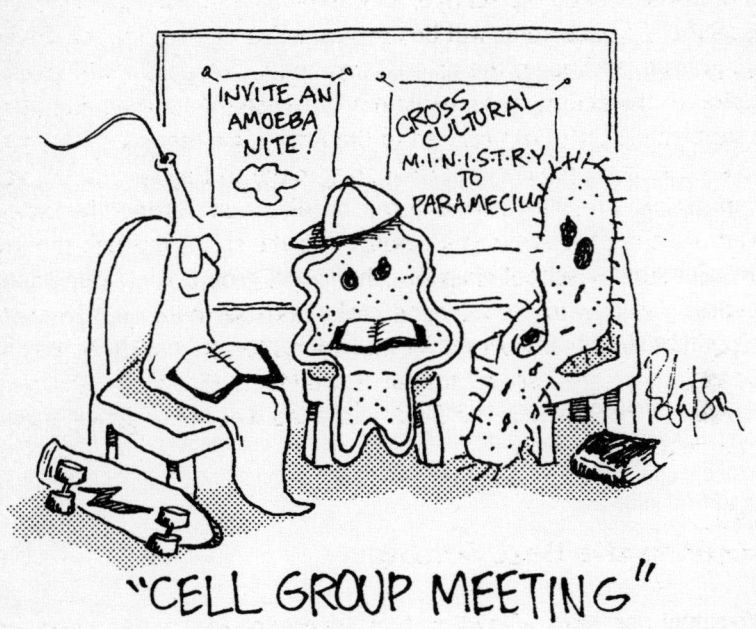

"CELL GROUP MEETING"

SESSION ONE

Choose to Believe Christ Will Make a Way for You Through the Maze

Facilitator: *Open your group with prayer, asking the Holy Spirit to come and minister to each person in your group.*

1. The content of our discussions in our small group is important, but enjoying the relationships is just as important. So we want to spend a little time today getting acquainted.

    Go around your group and give your name and see if you can remember a time when you were really lost and could not find your way. Tell about it briefly. If you're one of those people who never get lost, just share your name.

2. Picture a maze with a mouse frantically running around, sometimes bumping into a wall, sometimes standing dazed, and then trying again to find its way out. As a group, list all the feelings you think you would experience if you were in that maze trying to find your way.

3. Now list some times when life seemed confusing and you felt as if you couldn't figure it out or find your way through. A recent example for me (Marilyn) was when I received a letter from my first spiritual mentor, now a missionary, only a few years older than I am, who had just been diagnosed with cancer. One aspect of the maze was that I was being confronted with the reality that serious illness can strike anyone, even the deeply spiritual. The other factor that caused me to feel in the maze was the reality that I'm getting close to the age when serious illness is more common. I felt uncertain and confused when I received his letter. What are some of your examples?

Copyright © 1995 The Chapel Ministries, Inc. Permission is granted to reproduce this session for members of a single small group. Each small group leader should have a purchased copy of this guide.

4. Think of some of the most confusing mazes you've faced or are facing currently in your life. Were the feelings associated with those experiences similar to the ones you described above for the mouse in the maze? Explain.

What did you do at those times? What actions did you take to deal with feelings such as fear, confusion, anxiety, or anger?

What feelings are the opposite of those you listed above?

5. What seems to be our perception of God when we're in a maze, living through a confusing time?

Read Psalm 6:1–3 (see questions below); 10:1; 13:1–2; 22:1–2; 38:1–2, 21; 43:1–2; 54:1–2; 55:1–8. After each passage is read, answer the following three questions:

a. What is the psalmist feeling?
b. What do you guess might be the nature of the writer's current situation?
c. What seems to be the psalmist's perception of God at the moment?

Now think about one of your confusing times. How similar or how different is your experience from the psalmist's?

6. Most of the above psalms are by David. In many of his psalms he is full of praise and sees the majesty and goodness of God. David knew God, but in confusing times what happened to his perception of God? Why?

The passages we've just read are prayers. Let's look back at these psalms and see what happens to the psalmist's perception of God after talking to him face-to-face. Read Psalm 10:16–18; 13:5–6; 22:3–5; 38:15; 43:4–5; 54:4; 55:22–23.

What happened between the early verses in the psalms we read for question 5 above and the later ones we just read?

The situations have not changed. What has changed? How did that happen?

Oswald Chambers puts it this way: "The meaning of prayer is that we get hold of God, not of the answer." (*My Utmost for His Highest*, New York: Dodd, Mead & Company, 1965. February 7 reading) What do you think about that concept? What does it mean to "get hold of God"?

7. What changed the psalmist was being in communion with God in honest, face-to-face dialogue. Read Psalm 38:9. This shows the depth of intimacy. After the psalmist shares his true feelings and then listens to God, God reveals his true self, and the psalmist is at peace again.

Does being in uncertain times always lead to uncertainty about God? Why or why not?

8. Being certain of God doesn't mean we won't feel confusion or fear, frustration or anger. But we can go immediately to him and find he is our certainty in uncertain times. Read Hebrews 4:14–16. For what reason does this scripture say we can boldly approach God?

When does it say we are to come?

When Jesus was in the Garden of Gethsemane praying "take this cup from me," apparently he was feeling uncertain. When he shouted, quoting Psalm 22, from the cross, "My God, My God, why have you forsaken me?" he expressed uncertainty. Yet in both instances he was totally submissive to the Father and certain of the Father's goodness and power and love. His feelings of uncertainty were springing from his human nature. The key is that just as he went face-to-face to the Father, so can we. That's what Hebrews 4:16 tells us to do.

If you had to put a number on the degree to which you can come directly to God with your uncertainty, what number would you say expresses where you are today? (Zero means never and 10 means always.) Explain your answer.

9. "Spiritual life is the life of a child. We are not uncertain of God, but uncertain of what He is going to do next." (*My Utmost for His Highest*, April 29) Children are trusting unless they learn it isn't safe. Just as Jesus cried *Abba* ("Daddy," "Papa") in Mark 14:36, so we are told that we, because of what Jesus did on the cross, can cry *Abba* too. We can come in childlike trust to our Father when we need him. Read Mark 14:36, Romans 8:15, and Galatians 4:6.

We are to bring our uncertainty in insecure times to the changeless and certain God. Read Hebrews 13:8. What does this mean to you?

10. *Close your session together in a time of prayer, praying brief, simple, sentence prayers. The key to true prayer is that it is face-to-face. Focus on the God you are addressing. Talk to God about the uncertainties you are facing and pray for others in the group and for the sessions ahead. When it seems like time to close, announce that you'll close by reading together the 50-Day Adventure "I Believe" Prayer, using Romans 8:28 as your promise verse and using the plural rather than the singular pronoun.*

> Father,
> Sometimes we feel confused and don't understand why things happen the way they do.
> Yet we believe you love us deeply, and absolutely nothing is beyond your control.
> Help us to live each day with confidence, trusting in the great promises of your Word.
> Today we are reminded: "In all things God works for the good of those who love him."
> Thank you for giving us the strength to be "I believe" people.
> Amen.

NOTES

SESSION TWO

Embrace the Great Promises of God's Word

1. Go around your group, reviewing your names and sharing one challenge you had in your life this week. Feel the support the sharing of common experiences brings, as you get to know each other's stresses in life.

Begin your group with the "I Believe" Prayer. Pray it as you did last week incorporating Romans 8:28 (or another verse if you like) and using the plural pronoun. As you read it together, focus on the person of the Lord to whom you are speaking. In order to switch gears from your fast-paced, challenge-filled lives, take a moment to quiet yourselves. Then pray:

> Father,
> Sometimes we feel confused and don't understand why things happen the way they do.
> Yet we believe you love us deeply, and absolutely nothing is beyond your control.
> Help us to live each day with confidence, trusting in the great promises of your Word.
> Today we are reminded: "In all things God works for the good of those who love him."
> Thank you for giving us the strength to be "I believe" people.
> Amen.

2. Our "I Believe" Prayer says our confidence comes from trusting the great promises of the Word of God. As a group, list as many promises from the Bible as you can think of.

Copyright © 1995 The Chapel Ministries, Inc. Permission is granted to reproduce this session for members of a single small group. Each small group leader should have a purchased copy of this guide.

Are you satisfied with how well you know the Bible's promises? Explain.

What happens in your mind when you are faced with a challenge or problem in life? Do fear-provoking images and thoughts come to mind? Or do you dwell on the promises of the Scriptures? Share what enters your mind at these times. (For example: a difficult time at work can result in the fear of losing your job.)

3. Read John 8:42–44. What was Jesus saying to the Jews about the devil?

When we're facing a troubling situation, we often think negative thoughts about the outcome or focus on our inadequacies. We may even impose ill motives on God or others. Though sometimes our sense of a situation is realistic, often it is not. Our own history, our own sin nature, and the lies of the evil one keep us stuck. Our greatest need is for truth. Have each of the following scriptures read. After each is read, give the truth that is stated there:

    a. John 14:16–18

What is the promise of Jesus here? What is the truth stated here?

Once we have received Jesus as our Savior, we may feel alone at times, but that is not the truth.

    b. John 14:27

What is the promise of Jesus here? What is the truth stated here?

We may at times feel like it is impossible to have peace, but that is not the truth.

   c. Colossians 2:13–15. Read that in at least two translations.

In New Testament times a victorious army would parade their prisoners of war through town. The image we see is of Christ the victor dragging a defeated Satan and his armies of demons, his prisoners of the won war. Here is this passage from *The Message:* "When you were stuck in your old sin-dead life, you were incapable of responding to God. God brought you alive—right along with Christ! Think of it! All sins forgiven, the slate wiped clean, that old arrest warrant canceled and nailed to Christ's Cross. He stripped all the spiritual tyrants in the universe of their sham authority at the Cross and marched them naked through the streets."

What promises do you see here?

Have a volunteer read this aloud and then read it aloud together:

- I am alive in Christ, and I can respond to God.
- I am forgiven, my slate wiped clean.
- My accusers are empty-handed.
- Jesus is the victor and he lives in me.
- I humbly thank you, Lord Christ.

Sometimes we focus on our failures and forget the truth that the gospel isn't about what we are, but about what God has done for us. What in the Colossians 2 passage we just read is most joy-producing to you?

   d. 1 John 1:5–10

What truths do you hear here?

Based on this passage, what are ways we could be living in the darkness?

How does walking in the darkness affect our closeness to other believers? Why?

Why is claiming to be without sin deceiving ourselves? Why is that dangerous?

What does *confession* mean?

What happens to the truths of God's Word when we refuse to own up to the reality of sin in our lives? See verse 10.

So sometimes the reason that truth, which can release us from anxiety and fear, is not powerful in our lives is because we're sinning and not taking responsibility for our sin. We're deceiving ourselves, hiding instead of owning up, not seeing the sin as God does, which, if we viewed it his way, would result in repentance.

4. In question 2 above, we talked about what goes on in our minds when we're facing a confusing maze, a challenge, a problem in life. We often think very negative thoughts. In place of those images of disasters and worst-case scenarios, what would happen if you thought about the Lord, the Good Shepherd, walking with you, or pictured his ministering angels with you in your place of fear? What other mental pictures might be helpful?

Probably the most powerful promise in the Word of God to us is: God is with us no matter what happens. If we would focus on that truth instead of on the disasters we imagine, how would that affect us?

5. We're going to close our group time by focusing on the promise of the presence of God—his very person with us. Read each of these scriptures out loud and then restate or paraphrase the truth you read there.

   a. Hebrews 13:5–6

   b. Deuteronomy 31:6,8

   c. Deuteronomy 20:3–4

   d. Psalm 23:4

Eugene Peterson in *The Message* translates this passage like this: "Even when the way goes through Death Valley, I'm not afraid when you walk at my side. Your trusty shepherd's crook makes me feel secure."

    e. John 16:32

Jesus knew that even his disciples would scatter when he needed them most. But the Father would remain with him. The only thing that ever separated Jesus from the presence of the Father was taking our sin upon himself. Read Matthew 27:45–51.

When Jesus called out in agony, "My God, my God, why have you forsaken me?" it was because at that moment he completely carried our sin and the Holy Father had to look away. At the same time, the veil of the temple, a four-inch-thick tapestry separating the Holy of Holies, in which the presence of God resided, was torn from top to bottom—indicating that nothing can ever separate us from God again as long as we are in Christ. The scripture below will reinforce that truth.

    f. Romans 8:38–39

List all the things in life that have no power to separate us from the God who loves us. Have you included the challenge you shared or thought about in the beginning of this session?

6. This week when you find yourself thinking fear-provoking thoughts, turn your mind to the truths of the Scriptures. Write down some of the verses we've talked about as well as the promises in your 50-Day Adventure journal. Read them over and over again. Fill your mind with truth. Simply by choosing to read them over and over again you will memorize them.

Close your group with a time of worship of the God of so many wonderful promises. Read Hebrews 13:15: "Through Him then, let us continually offer up a sacrifice of praise to God, that is, the fruit of lips that give thanks to His name" (NASB).

③ SESSION THREE

Pursue Support Relationships with Other Believers

1. *This is our third week together. We're talking today about the importance of relationships in our spiritual journey, especially in times of confusion or pressure. Go around your group and do this word association. It may be that many of you will give the same word; that's fine. The goal is to share responses, not to come up with a list of several different ones.*

What word or phrase comes to your mind when you hear the word *support*?

What words or phrases are the opposite of *support* for you?

What did we just learn about support and our feelings associated with it?

2. Probably one of the opposites of support we think of is the word *alone*. In the Adventure journal this week we'll be looking at Ecclesiastes 4:9–12. Read that passage aloud now.

What are the benefits of togetherness listed by the author?

Copyright © 1995 The Chapel Ministries, Inc. Permission is granted to reproduce this session for members of a single small group. Each small group leader should have a purchased copy of this guide.

Take a few minutes to talk about how you are doing in your daily journal. How well is it going and what are some things you are learning? If you've skipped some days, just start again this week.

3. In the journal this week (p. 36) we'll also find questions referring to something Jesus told the disciples about community. Let's take some time to think about and remember what the New Testament tells us regarding our importance to each other in the body of Christ, our community with one another. What teachings concerning these relationships can you recall?

Read Acts 2:41–47.

Three thousand people responded that day on the streets in front of the temple. What happened after that in the lives of these people?

To what activities was the early church devoted?

Where did they meet?

About how many people would you guess came to each house?

List as many adjectives as you can to describe the kind of community that existed among the believers in these homes. What do you think a believer would have done when going through a confusing time in his or her life?

These believers undoubtedly gave and received much support from one another. Compare that to your experience in the church today. Do you feel a close, deep connection with other believers, or do you feel more like "ships passing" when you see one another? Explain your answer.

4. The New Testament is full of commands concerning how we are supposed to give and receive support from one another. Have a different volunteer read each Scripture below:

   a. 1 Thessalonians 5:11

What does it mean to "build each other up"?

How well would you have to know someone to let that person truly "build" you up? Explain.

   b. 1 Thessalonians 4:18

The Message says, "Reassure one another with these words." What words is the author (Paul) referring to?

What characterizes a relationship in which you can encourage someone going through a confusing time by pointing to the Second Coming of Christ?

How would this kind of reassuring fit into your usual conversations with people from your church?

c. James 5:16

What kinds of sins do you imagine those believers confessed to each other when they asked for prayer and healing from the effects of their sin?

Read Ephesians 4:29–32. What kinds of struggles with sin are listed here?

In which of these areas could you ask for prayer today?

We don't always do enough of this kind of supporting of one another. As a result, we stand alone, struggling with sin common to us all, rather than being in the safe support of other believers. Why do you think that is?

What do you think can be done about the lack of support in this area?

d. 1 Peter 1:22; John 13:34–35; Romans 12:10

How do we do what these verses tell us to do?

e. 1 Peter 5:8–9

Notice that the command in verse 6, "Humble yourselves," is plural. These verses are written to a close-knit group of believers. They weren't to try to stand alone. Together they were to be alert for evil. Together they were to resist temptation. How do you resist temptation with another person?

f. Galatians 5:13

How do we fulfill this command?

5. We live in a very individualistic culture. How has this affected us in the church?

When was the last time you sought prayer and support and shared a real need with a fellow believer?

When was the last time you prayed with another believer?

6. One of our action steps for this Adventure is to "Unleash the Power of Prayer Partnerships" by meeting four times to pray with another Christian during the 50 days (p. 9 in the Adult Journal). What has been your experience with prayer partnerships?

In the book *Two Are Better Than One* by David Mains and Steve Bell (Shippensburg, Pennsylvania: Destiny Image, 1995. p. 10–11), we find this helpful insight about one of the values of praying with others:

"Spending time with someone else in the presence of God enhances personal times with him. You become practiced and more comfortable in his presence. Talking with the Lord about specific issues in your life no longer seems so abstract. On top of that, many have testified that the promises of Scripture come alive to them in a whole new way. What had become the drudgery of doing basic spiritual disciplines is transformed into a new spiritual vitality."

How many of us already have a prayer partner for the Adventure? The prayer group can include two or three people. Is there anyone here who is looking for a partner? Perhaps some from our group would like to team up.

7. *Close your group tonight with a longer period of prayer. Share requests and pray for one another.*

④ SESSION FOUR

Look for the Joys That Refresh Your Spirit

1. *There is a book called* Happiness Is a Choice. *Go around your group and tell to what extent you agree or disagree (zero percent meaning not at all; 100 percent meaning full agreement). Give a one-sentence explanation for your reason.*

The book is actually about depression. The concept is that even when we're depressed or going through a confusing time, we can choose our attitude. That's not easy to do. What are some factors that hold us in fear or depression when life is difficult?

2. Read the following passages and notice Paul's perspective in these situations:

   a. 2 Corinthians 1:8. What is Paul feeling?

   Read verse 10. What is Paul's attitude?

   b. 2 Corinthians 7:5. What is Paul feeling?

It is evident that Paul is not denying his painful feelings. He feels them and takes them to God and to others for support and then he chooses his attitude.

Copyright © 1995 The Chapel Ministries, Inc. Permission is granted to reproduce this session for members of a single small group. Each small group leader should have a purchased copy of this guide.

Read verse 4. What is Paul's chosen attitude?

When we are going through a confusing time, we have feelings that we need to process, to experience, to share with others and with God for support.

Read verse 6 in the same passage. How does God comfort Paul?

Read Psalm 62:8. What is God telling us to do here?

3. So even when we are going through a confusing time and feeling scared or angry, hurt or depressed, we can still choose an attitude of hope and trust. Read these passages, restate the commands, and explain how you could fulfill these commands when you're in the midst of confusing times.

   a. 1 Thessalonians 5:16,18

   b. Philippians 4:4–8

   c. Psalm 103:2

4. The issue is one of focus. We've all heard that half a glass of water can be viewed as being half full or half empty—even though it's the same half a glass. What does that mean?

In the Philippians 4:4–8 passage we just read, it says that even when we feel anxious we can choose to focus on all that God has done (giving thanks). Read the following passages, considering where God wants us to fix our attention, what we should choose to focus our mind on:

a. Isaiah 26:3

How do you keep your mind "steadfastly" on God? Where does it tend to wander?

b. 2 Corinthians 10:5

If we don't take captive our thoughts, we become the captive of our thoughts. How?

Have you ever felt captive of a negative thought pattern, especially in a confusing time? What did you do?

How do you take captive your thoughts?

God doesn't command us to do things that are impossible for us, so no matter how confusing life gets, we can still choose where to focus our thoughts and attention. How do you feel about the proposition that God is holding us accountable for what we choose to concentrate our thoughts on?

Read Psalm 9:1–2.

The Amplified Bible says, "I will praise You, O Lord, with my whole heart; I will show forth (recount and tell aloud) all Your marvelous works and wonderful deeds! I will rejoice in You and be in high spirits; I will sing praise to your name, O Most High!"

With what is the psalmist saying he chooses to fill his thoughts?

What results when he fills his thoughts with these things?

5. Sometimes we get so wrapped up in confusion we forget the good things that happen. We are so concerned about our struggles, our worries, our doubts, that we miss the joys. When we take time to see the positives, we gain strength to deal with the negatives. This is not just some kind of "positive thinking" gimmick, to look at life through rose-colored glasses. We want to look at life realistically, but we want to make sure we don't miss the blessings God keeps sending our way.

Take some time now in your group for everyone to share briefly one challenge or struggle in his or her life this week. Afterwards have each person share one joy.

Doing this in our group today will reinforce the fourth Adventure action step—"Energize Your Faith by Tracking Daily Joys." In the journal on pages 40–41, the Daily Joy Tracker provides a place for you to list them. What value do you see in this exercise?

6. How are you doing in your prayer partnerships? What difficulties have you encountered?

In what ways have these partnerships been valuable to you?

7. *Close your group with prayer. Begin with intercession, mentioning some of the things people shared as their challenges this week. Then spend the rest of the time in thanksgiving to God, so that you conclude by focusing on the joys of your life.*

SESSION FIVE

Remove Unnecessary Confusion from Your Life

1. *Our action step this week is to find some ways to unclutter our lives. When you hear the word* clutter, *what comes to mind? Go around the group and each share one association with clutter; several of you may have similar ideas—the goal is not to make an exhaustive list, but to share your own thoughts.*

   What are some opposites of *clutter?*

   How would you describe an uncluttered life?

   If you were going to start uncluttering your life, where would you start?

2. A medical doctor, Richard A. Swenson, has written a powerful book called *Margin,* the subtitle of which is: *Restoring Emotional, Physical, Financial, and Time Reserves to Overloaded Lives.* (Colorado Springs: NavPress, 1992.) We could say that the uncluttered life is a life with margin. What do you think he means by margin?

Copyright © 1995 The Chapel Ministries, Inc. Permission is granted to reproduce this session for members of a single small group. Each small group leader should have a purchased copy of this guide.

How much margin do you imagine the average Christian has?

On pages 83–87, Swenson lists 23 kinds of "overload" in our lives: activity, change, choice, commitment, competition, debt, decision, education, expectation, fatigue, hurry, information, media, ministry, noise, people, pollution, possession, problem, technology, traffic, waste, and work. Which of these do you identify as an area of overload in your life?

3. What difference does the degree of overload we have in some of these areas make when we are going through a confusing time in our lives?

The middle of a confusing time may not be the best time to evaluate our overload or degree of margin. Do you think this is true? Why or why not?

We need to be reevaluating all the time, not waiting for pain to be our only motivator. What else could motivate us to take a good hard look at our lives, checking for overload and inspiring action?

Read Matthew 6:25–34. Then read verse 33 in as many translations as you have in your group.
Here are verses 32–34 from *The Message*:
"People who don't know God and the way he works fuss over these things, but you know both God and how he works. Steep your life in God-reality, God-initiative, God-provisions. Don't worry about missing out. You'll find all your everyday human concerns will be met.

"Give your entire attention to what God is doing right now, and don't get worked up about what may or may not happen tomorrow. God will help you deal with whatever hard things come up when the time comes."

How does *The Message* express "Seek first the kingdom of God"?

How do you do that?

To be more aware of God than what's going on around you is a challenge. How does this relate to uncluttering your life? (See Action Step 5, Adult Journal, p. 11.)

4. Read Isaiah 59:2 in as many translations as you have.
Sin is a major source of clutter. How does sin greatly complicate a confusing time?

Read Isaiah 59:1–15. List all the kinds of sins mentioned; with each give modern words that express how we sin in the very same ways.

Whenever we are going through a confusing or difficult time, we need to begin dealing with it by examining ourselves and looking for unconfessed sin. What do we sometimes do instead?

What does the word *repentance* mean to you?

5. Read each of the five situations one at a time and then answer the following three questions after each one:
- If this person were first to attend to repentance to see if any is needed, what possible sins might he or she check for? (Your answer may be "none" in some cases.)
- What kind of clutter may have contributed to the current problem and confusion? (Your answer may be "none" in some cases.)
- After considering the areas of sin and clutter, what would you suggest the person do next?

Jim and Judy have been married for 14 years. Jim owns his own business, and this takes a lot of his time and energy. He is very committed to his church, and his position as deacon consumes much of his discretionary time. For several months, Judy has been expressing unhappiness with their life together. She feels neglected and angry. Jim feels she's being unreasonable and self-centered.

Apply the questions to Jim.

Liz and Tom are working on their bills. They've just written checks to Commonwealth Edison, Visa, Discover, Ameritech, First Card, and to the Thompson Bank, which holds their mortgage. They've been married for two and a half years, and they're beginning to notice that although they both earn a good salary, there is less and less money left over at the end of the month. They would like to go on vacation this summer but will not be able to afford it.

Karen is a single mom with three children ages 15, 14, and 10. She received a call from the school today stating that her 15-year-old was reading a pornographic magazine in study hall. She is very upset.

Apply the questions to Karen.

The company Linda works for was sold to new management six months ago. All supervisory personnel were replaced. Linda met with her boss this morning for her first review under the new management. She was told she works too slowly. She is very upset, having worked for the firm for 11 years with consistently good reviews. She is feeling helpless.

Cal is furious. He's served on the "Toys for Kids" committee for two years. The recognition banquet was last night and his name was not mentioned, even though it was his idea that was used in all the publicity.

6. Another major block to dealing effectively with confusion or clutter in our lives is forgetting who God really is. How does that block us?

What are some things we think about God when we're going through troubles? How does Satan use our doubts about God?

What do you do when you're in the middle of a confusing time and you have doubts or questions about God?

Read Psalm 62:5–8.

What is David telling us to do here?

What does it mean to you to pour out your heart to him?

Read Psalm 34:1–6.

The Message has a fresh paraphrase of verses 5–6: "Look at him; give him your warmest smile. Never hide your feelings from him. When I was desperate, I called out, and Yahweh got me out of a tight spot."

The phrase in verse 5 in the *New American Standard Bible,* "their faces shall never be ashamed," is "never hide your feelings from him" in *The Message.* Shame about our feelings can keep us from going to God face-to-face and being with him when we're doubting his care, his goodness, his power. Yet we see the psalmist often sharing these kinds of doubts with God directly. What do you feel when you think of yourself telling God your doubts about him when in the middle of a confusing time?

Perhaps the greatest evidence of faith in God is telling him truly what you feel, even when you have doubts or questions toward him. What do you think of that idea?

7. *Close your group with a time of sentence prayers, praying for yourself and one another about the ways you see you need to unclutter your life.*

SESSION SIX

Accept the Lord's Grace and Forgiveness

Facilitator: Begin your group with prayer, asking the Holy Spirit to come and be with you and teach you.

1. Go around your group, each of you completing this sentence:

Lately, God has been saying to me . . .

- keep on target in my life
- change my priorities
- reach for the best
- cut out the excess baggage
- let go of destructive habits
- don't turn back
- run with determination
- keep my eyes on Christ
- turn away from sin
- other_____

2. In *The Pursuit of God*, A.W. Tozer declares, "All our heartaches and a great many of our physical ills spring directly out of our sins. Pride, arrogance, resentfulness, evil imaginings, malice, greed are the sources of more human pain than all the diseases that ever afflicted mortal flesh." (Camp Hill, Pennsylvania: Christian Publications, Inc., 1982. p. 110) What do you think of his idea?

There is no doubt there are some mazes of life and confusing times that we have somehow created by our own unwise or sinful choices. List as many of those kinds of situations as you can.

_{Copyright © 1995 The Chapel Ministries, Inc. Permission is granted to reproduce this session for members of a single small group. Each small group leader should have a purchased copy of this guide.}

Now list some problem situations (mazes or confusing times) a person could be in that are clearly not a result of personal choices or one's own sin. (Some situations are a combination of factors.)

3. When we realize that the mess we're in is the consequence of our own disobedience to God, what can we do?

Can you think of some times in your life when you've been in this situation? What did you do?

4. What happens in our relationship with God and our feelings toward him when we realize that the maze we're in was created by ignoring him and his ways?

Read Psalm 119:65–67, 71–72.

What does the psalmist seem to be experiencing?

How has he responded to seeing his wrong?

Read Psalm 119:75–77, 80.

The psalmist's affliction or problem seems to have turned him back to God and taught him something. What?

5. Sometimes we react to affliction, even affliction that is self-generated, in another way. In what other ways might we react toward God? Read Proverbs 19:3.

Why would a person react this way?

6. Taking responsibility is not always easy. What is the opposite of taking responsibility?

Blaming others or seeing oneself as a victim of circumstances is a common way of dealing with problems in life that are actually the result of our own choices to ignore God and his ways. Read 1 John 1:5–9.

What other way of not taking responsibility is mentioned here?

7. Denial is a common way of dealing with sin. How does God want us to deal with it?

What would you think about a person who confessed a sin and then turned around and chose to do the same thing again, assuming that God is forgiving and would forgive him or her?

Read Romans 6:15. Comment on how this verse relates to the question above.

8. To confess means to repent as well. I'm not really confessing if I'm intending to do the same thing again. Confessing means to agree with God, to see the situation and myself as he does. It means to take full responsibility for what I have done and to humbly ask God for forgiveness while wanting to turn away from the sin totally. Read Psalm 32:1–5.

Describe David's life (verses 3–4) while he was in denial.

Now read all of Psalm 32 below from *The Message*:

Count yourself lucky, how happy you must be—
  you get a fresh start,
  your slate's wiped clean.

Count yourself lucky—
  Yahweh holds nothing against you
  and you're holding nothing back from him.

When I kept it all inside,
  my bones turned to powder,
  my words became daylong groans.

The pressure never let up;
  all the juices of my life dried up.

Then I let it all out;
  I said, "I'll make a clean breast of my failures to Yahweh."

Suddenly the pressure was gone—
  my guilt dissolved,
  my sin disappeared.

These things add up. Every one of us needs to pray;
  when all hell breaks loose and the dam bursts
  we'll be on high ground, untouched.

Yahweh's my island hideaway,
  keeps danger far from the shore,
  throws garlands of hosannas around my neck.

Let me give you some good advice;
  I'm looking you in the eye
  and giving it to you straight:

"Don't be ornery like a horse or mule
  that needs bit and bridle
  to stay on track."

God-defiers are always in trouble;
  Yahweh-affirmers find themselves loved
  every time they turn around.

Celebrate Yahweh.
  Sing together—everyone!
  All you honest hearts, raise the roof!

In which verse above do you find the most personal meaning? *Go around your group and each read that meaningful verse and very briefly share why.*

9. When we repent and confess, God gives us his forgiveness totally. Our closeness to him is restored. Remember the prodigal son in Luke 15 (verses 11–31)? What kind of welcome was he expecting from the father?

What kind of welcome did he receive?

The restoration of the relationship came when the son returned to his father in honesty and took responsibility for his sin and lack of wisdom. That didn't mean his inheritance would be restored. He had blown it. But more importantly his relationship with his father was restored.

Let's close our group tonight in a minute or so of silence. This will give you a chance to talk to God about anything you need to. Then plan to take repentant action.

Facilitator: *After the period of silence, begin a time of brief sentence prayers. Encourage those who so choose to pray out loud.*

THE COMMUNION CHANNEL

NOTES

SESSION SEVEN

Discover How Jesus Identifies with Your Struggles

Facilitator: *Discuss with your group whether they would like to continue meeting when this series is completed.*

1. Let's open our group with a brief time of prayer, asking the Lord to speak to us and to make his presence known among us as we talk about how he identifies with our struggles.

2. Think of what you know from Scripture of Jesus the man. How would you describe him: physically, emotionally, relationally? What do you perceive him to have been like? Describe his personality and how he related. When you can, give evidence from the Bible.

3. The Adult Journal brings us to four important passages regarding the manhood and human suffering of Jesus. We'll be referring to those later, but there is another very key passage found in Hebrews 5:1–10. Have a volunteer read that from a translation such as the *New International Version* or *New American Standard Bible*.

What is the responsibility of the high priest as described in verse 1?

In order to fulfill this responsibility a priest must be qualified in two ways as explained in verses 2 and 4. What are these qualifications?

_{Copyright © 1995 The Chapel Ministries, Inc. Permission is granted to reproduce this session for members of a single small group. Each small group leader should have a purchased copy of this guide.}

How does the passage state that Jesus is qualified (stated here in reverse order)?

4. Have a volunteer read the passage again from *The Message* below:

> Every high priest selected to represent men and women before God and offer sacrifices for their sins should be able to deal gently with their failings, since he knows what it's like from his own experience. But that also means that he has to offer sacrifices for his own sins as well as the people's.
>
> No one elects himself to this honored position. He's called to it by God, as Aaron was. Neither did Christ presume to set himself up as high priest, but was set apart by the One who said to him, "You're my Son; today I celebrate you!" In another place God declares, "You're a priest forever in the royal order of Melchizedek."
>
> While he lived on earth, anticipating death, Jesus cried out in pain and wept in sorrow as he offered up priestly prayers to God. Because he honored God, God answered him. Though he was God's Son, he learned trusting-obedience by what he suffered, just as we do. Then, having arrived at the full stature of his maturity and having been announced by God as high priest in the order of Melchizedek, he became the source of eternal salvation to all who believingly obey him.

The calling of Jesus into this high priestly position of being the one who represents us to God requires the approval of the Father. We see this in Matthew 3:16–17. Read that passage and relate it to the passage above (Hebrews 5:1–10).

5. In verse 2 of Hebrews, chapter 5, we find the other very important qualification of a high priest. Describe in detail what you think *gently* means, using other insights from the passage which throw light on the meaning. Include your own thoughts as well.

Describe what you think a priest who did not have this quality would be like.

We're going to call on the Greek experts for some help with the word meaning here. William Barclay says this: "The priest must be bound up with men in the bundle of life. In connection with this he used a wonderful word—*metriopathein*. We have translated it *to feel gently*. . . . The Greeks defined *metriopatheia* (the corresponding noun) as the mean between extravagant grief and utter indifference. It was feeling about men in the right way. . . . *patience* . . . the child of *metriopathei*. . . . It is a wonderful word. It means the ability not to lose one's temper with people when they are foolish and will not learn and do the same thing over and over again." (*The Letter to the Hebrews*, Revised Edition, Philadelphia: The Westminster Press, 1976. pp. 46–47)

Think of some examples of people who are suffering. How would you respond to them if you felt "extravagant grief"?

How would you respond to them in "utter indifference"?

The necessary quality the priest must have lies between these two extremes. Barclay says patience is the child of this midway point, which the scripture calls "dealing gently." How does being at this midway point lead to a loving patience as you listen to the suffering one?

The Book of Hebrews tells us that Jesus is right there. He is actually the only one in the universe who can "deal gently" with us in the purest form. Why is this?

6. Read again Hebrews 5:2.

Who is the priest supposed to deal gently with?

What gives him the ability to deal gently with them?

We need some help in understanding how Jesus can possibly identify with us when we're tempted and suffering through a confusing time. Two passages we read in our journal this week will help us here. Read Hebrews 2:14–18.

How does this passage state that Jesus is like us?

The other passage is Hebrews 4:14–16. From what is stated here, how is Jesus like us?

We need some help in understanding the word *weakness*. We know it cannot mean sin since Jesus never sinned. Larry Richards says this:

> This verse is often misunderstood. . . . Weakness does not refer to our human tendency to give in to temptation, but to our capacity to feel it! Our weakness is human frailty itself: the hungers, the desires, the pains to which we are subject and which push and pull against our wills. Jesus, in taking on human nature, took on our weaknesses as well. At every point in every way, Jesus was tested as we are. In fact, he was tempted beyond the point at which we give in.

Richards then gives an example of two prisoners of war, one which, after two months of torture, yields. The other resists for years even though the pressures increase.

> Both learned something of their weakness as the pressures grew. But only the one who continued to resist really knew how weak he was, as he daily had to cope with and overcome his human frailty. Only the one who

continued to resist understood the full weight of pain that being a human being involves. And this is what the Bible says about Jesus. He knows more about human frailty than we do. He really understands how terrible it is to be weak. And because he understands, he is able to sympathize with us when we find ourselves tempted. He even understands the agony of dying. (*The Teacher's Commentary,* Wheaton, Illinois: Victor Books, 1987. pp. 999–1000)

A word that comes to my mind that seems similar to weakness is human vulnerability.

Think about a maze or confusing time you're in now or have been in recently. Think of all the fears, inadequacies, and weakness you've experienced. Then think about Jesus in the Garden of Gethsemane. Read Hebrews 5:7. How do you think he felt?

What similarities can you find between what you experienced and felt and Jesus' "prayers and petitions with loud cries and tears"?

What does it mean to you that Jesus was wholly human?

7. Read Hebrews 5:8 in as many translations as you have among you and then read it here in the contemporary English translation *The Message:* "Though he was God's Son, he learned trusting-obedience by what he suffered."

What do you think this passage means?

What does it mean to you that Jesus "learned" obedience?

Read Philippians 2:8.

What does it mean to you that Jesus "became" obedient?

The Greek phrase "He learned from what he suffered," is a Greek proverb, meaning "Learning comes from suffering." What was Jesus' way of dealing with suffering according to Hebrews 5:7–8?

What is the opposite of "reverent submission"?

Richards says, "We never benefit from our trials or sufferings when we react rebelliously or in panic. God seeks to strengthen us through every experience of life. Meeting life with reverent submission frees us from being overwhelmed, and helps us grow in our own ability to feel with those who are hurt. . . ." (*The Teacher's Commentary*) What do you think would help you meet life with reverent submission?

8. *Spend a little time briefly sharing what your greatest need is today. Then pray by name for one another.*

SESSION EIGHT

Place Your Hope in the God of Surprising Outcomes

Facilitator: *Spend some time discussing whether the group wants to continue meeting, whether you're going to take a break before meeting again, what new materials you will need, and where you will meet.*

1. We're going to begin our group with the "I Believe" Prayer, praying in the plural. We'll use the last promise in the Adult Journal, 1 Corinthians 1:25. (Or use another verse of your choice.)

> *Father,*
> *Sometimes we feel confused and don't understand why things happen the way they do.*
> *Yet we believe you love us deeply, and absolutely nothing is beyond your control.*
> *Help us to live each day with confidence, trusting in the great promises of your Word.*
> *Today we are reminded that "the foolishness of God is wiser than man's wisdom, and the weakness of God is stronger than man's strength."*
> *Thank you for giving us the strength to be "I believe" people.*
> *Amen.*

2. What does it mean to you to put your hope in something or someone?

What do you feel when you think of putting your hope in something?

Which feels safer to you: putting your hope in yourself or in something outside of yourself?

Copyright © 1995 The Chapel Ministries, Inc. Permission is granted to reproduce this session for members of a single small group. Each small group leader should have a purchased copy of this guide.

Does the degree of hope you feel depend on the object of your hope, or do you think it has more to do with where you are within yourself?

3. In a wonderful book called *Yearning: Living Between How It Is and How It Ought to Be*, pastor and author M. Craig Barnes says, "The beginning place for this spirituality usually is the shattering of our earlier hopes for getting life together.... In the moment in which we feel abandoned by both our dreams and the God we thought would save them for us—in precisely that moment we are ready to receive God's true salvation. It is then we discover that God wants to save us, not our dreams.... A vast amount of energy goes into maintaining the hope that if only we will live as Christians, life can be as we have dreamed." (Downers Grove, Illinois: InterVarsity Press, 1991. pp. 21–22)

When we are in the middle of a confusing time, we often have an idea of how we would like God to work it out—it's a desire for his intervention, it's a part of our dream. When you think of the disciples seeing Jesus being carted off like a criminal, what do you think was their expectation of how God would work things out?

They probably did not believe that God would let Jesus die. "Yet as Job learned from the voice out of the whirlwind, we will never understand the ways of God.... In the forsakenness of Christ on the cross, it certainly seemed as if God had missed again. God did not spare his Son this bitterly hard part of the journey. If we call ourselves followers of Christ, we cannot expect God to save us from it, either." (*Yearning*, p. 26)

The disciples surely experienced disillusionment with God and with the way he works and doesn't work. What do you think they were feeling after Jesus died?

Read Luke 24:11.

What is the context? (If necessary, skim the surrounding verses.)

How open were the disciples at this point to the idea of Jesus' resurrection?

4. One of the important ways we can put our hope in God is to let go of our preconceived notions of how he is going to work in our behalf. As the disciples learned, he is the God of surprising outcomes. In fact, as Dan Allender puts it, "God is unpredictable. He will neither permit us to know our own future nor allow us to foresee when the Lord returns. There isn't any moment of life that we can look at and say: 'I know what God is going to do here, and how He is going to accomplish His will.' But it is possible to observe, participate, and marvel in the mystery of God." (Dr. Dan B. Allender and Dr. Temper Longman III, *Cry of the Soul,* Colorado Springs: NavPress, 1994. p. 222)

What the disciples learned of God's surprising outcomes developed their ability to sacrifice, endure, and trust. Later they would have opportunities to practice their faith in God. Read each passage below and answer these questions:

- What was the difficulty or challenge the disciples faced?
- How did they respond? (You may have to check the context to find this answer.)
- How do you see that hoping in the God of surprising outcomes helped them?

a. Acts 2:13 (see also verses 14–41)

b. Acts 2:44–45; 4:34–35

c. Acts 4:1–4 (see also verses 1–17)

d. Acts 4:18 (see also verses 19–22)

e. Acts 5:40 (see also verses 41–42)

5. We've seen above many challenges and confusing times: being ridiculed, being called on to give up private property, being thrown in jail, being told by religious leaders to stop talking about their faith and their God, and being beaten for no good reason. In any of these situations they could have had their own preconceived notions of how God should maneuver the outcome. But instead they let go and let God be God. How did the disciples come to this wonderful faith?

By yielding their desire to help Jesus avoid capture, giving up their dream of a Messiah to save them from Rome, suffering through Jesus' death, and meeting the resurrected Christ, the disciples witnessed quite the surprising outcome. We also need to journey through these phases to grow in faith. Think of one of your confusing times. Did you experience these phases and struggles? Share some examples.

6. Dan Allender says, "He [God] draws us to darkness and, in the midst of what appears awful, He shows something of his awe-full, bright goodness. God's methods are indeed mysterious. He is the eternal artist who orchestrates horizontal circumstances to provoke us to ask hard questions about Him. And, oddly, those questions invite us to know and trust Him with a depth unavailable without asking those questions." (*Cry of the Soul*, p. 223)

What questions do you remember asking during some of your confusing times?

Are there times when you are afraid to ask God your questions concerning him? Why?

We sometimes are taught that struggling with God is irreverent or unbelieving, yet we see the great men and women of God, even in the Scriptures, confronting God. It is a part of being intimate, and without that openness, our hope in God is shallow. "All suffering invites us to struggle with God. And the struggle with God gives us a glimpse of His character, seen in the paradox of the Cross. It is the suffering and resurrection of Christ that transforms the heart. . . . Doubt, confusion, even radical struggle are required before we are inclined to surrender to His goodness. Surrender is not possible without a fight." (*Cry of the Soul*, pp. 224–225)

What does it mean to you to surrender to God?

What would you say is the relationship between openly asking God your questions and sharing your feelings with him, and surrendering to him?

What would you say is the relationship between surrender and putting your hope in God?

7. Read Romans 15:13 in various translations.

What does this scripture say is the source of joy and peace?

Notice it doesn't say believing or trusting in *what,* but in *whom*—in the God who has shown himself trustworthy, the God of surprising outcomes. *Close by reading this scripture (below) together three times in a row. In the last reading, look at one another, giving this benediction as a gift to one another:*

"Oh! May the God of green hope fill you up with joy, fill you up with peace, so that your believing lives, filled with the life-giving energy of the Holy Spirit, will brim over with hope!"

(Romans 15:13, *The Message*)

LAST WORDS

We Want Your Comments

The Chapel Ministries wants to hear from you. We want your feedback as a leader and the comments of your group. We are especially interested in stories of how God worked through your small group experience. Write to us at:

The Chapel Ministries
Editorial Department
Box 30
Wheaton, IL 60189

Or send an e-mail with your comments to: T50DSA@aol.com

LAST MONTH MY MOTHER HAD A TRIPLE BY-PASS. WHEN SHE GOT OUT OF THE HOSPITAL, ALL THE NEIGHBORS BROUGHT FOOD, CLEANED HER HOUSE AND MADE LIFE-WELL-EASIER.

THEN AN UNBELIEVER THAT I WORK WITH HAD AN EMERGENCY OPERATION. ALL THEIR FRIENDS FILLED THE HOUSE WITH FOOD UNTIL HER HUSBAND BEGGED FOR THEM TO STOP.

THERE'S JUST ONE THING I DON'T UNDERSTAND.

HOW CAN THAT HAPPEN WHEN THEY'RE NOT IN A SMALL GROUP?

Small Group Resources from the Chapel

If you're leading a Bible study, Sunday school class, or small group through the 50-Day Adventure "What to Do When You Don't Know What to Do," here are the resources created to help you and the individuals in your group.

Adult Journal
What to Do When You Don't Know What to Do ($6.00)
Each individual needs a journal.

When Life Becomes a Maze by David Mains ($6.00/$12.00 audiobook)
Each household needs a copy of this book.

Believe It Or Not Scripture Promise Pack ($1.00)
A great way for individuals to embrace the promises of God's Word.

Adventure Orientation Video ($25.00)
The first part of this 85-minute video is an overview of the Adventure topics and action steps. The second part provides training on implementing the Adventure in different ministries of your church, including small groups.

Adventure Resource Video ($20.00)
Use this video in your small group to break the ice or to introduce the weekly topics. Included are productions of eight short dramas as well as Adventure segments from "You Need to Know."

Request your copies of these Chapel Ministries resources today. Use the order form on the next page for convenient delivery, or ask for these resources at your church or local Christian bookstore.

The Chapel Ministries Resources Order Form

What to Do When You Don't Know What to Do

Item	Title	Retail	Discount **see below	Quantity	Total
2610	Adult Journal	$6.00			
1761	When Life Becomes a Maze	$6.00			
				Subtotal	

** Quantity Discount
Total the 'Qty' columns for the above two items to determine your quantity discount price.
1–99: $4.80   100–299: $4.40   300+: $4.10

Item	Title	Retail	Discount	Total
7772	Believe It Or Not Scripture Promise Pack	$1.00		
450U	When Life Becomes a Maze audiobook	$12.00		
3607	Small Group Leader's Guide	$7.00		
8418	Adventure Orientation Video	$25.00	$20.00	
8421	Adventure Resource Video	$20.00	$15.00	
			Subtotal	

Other Adventures (Call The Chapel Ministries for quantity discounts on selected items.)

Item	Title	Retail	Total
5689	Facing Down Our Fears Adult Journal and How to Fear God Without Being Afraid of Him book	$10.00	
1723	Scared to Life book	$8.00	
5690	Daring to Dream Again Adult Journal and How to Be a World Class Christian book	$10.00	
1678	Never Too Late to Dream book	$8.00	
		Subtotal	
3505	Facing Down Our Fears Small Group Leader's Guide	$7.00	
3402	Daring to Dream Again Small Group Leader's Guide	$7.00	
		Subtotal	
		TOTAL	

Add 10% for UPS shipping/handling ($4.00 minimum)
Canadian or Illinois residents add 7% GST/sales tax
Total (subtotal + shipping + tax)
Here's my donation to help support the work of The Chapel Ministries

Ship my order to: **TOTAL AMOUNT ENCLOSED**

Name _____ Church Name _____
Street Address* _____ City _____
State/Prov _____ Zip/Code _____ Phone (___) _____
*(Note: UPS will not deliver to a PO box)

Mail this order form with your check made payable to:
The Chapel Ministries, Box 30, Wheaton, IL 60189-0030
In Canada: Box 2000, Waterdown, ON L0R 2H0

For U.S. Visa, MasterCard, or Discover card orders
call 1-800-224-2735.
In Canada call 1-800-461-4114.   SGLG96